The Five Snouts

poems by

C.M. Clark

Finishing Line Press
Georgetown, Kentucky

The Five Snouts

ACKNOWLEDGMENTS

"Starting in Xi'an" appears in Issue 6 of *The Lindenwood Review*.
"The Stuttering Emissaries of Turfan" appears in the *Metonym Literary Journal*.
"Dust. Sand. Earth. Silence" and "Afternoon" appear in *Dogwood: A Journal of
Poetry and Prose*.
"Twilight" will be appearing in a forthcoming edition of *Travellin' Mama*.

Publisher: Leah Maines

Editor: Christen Kincaid

Cover Art: "Castaways" © C.M. Clark, 1984

Author Photo: C.M. Clark

Cover Design: Elizabeth Maines McCleavy

Printed in the USA on acid-free paper.
Order online: www.finishinglinepress.com
Also available on amazon.com

Author inquiries and mail orders:
Finishing Line Press
P. O. Box 1626
Georgetown, Kentucky 40324
U. S. A.

Table of Contents

Requiem for a Headscarf 1

The Sleep Songs 3

Tirza & the Black Sisters 5

Dust. Sand. Earth. Silence. 7

Hope Is a Thing with Guidelines 8

Starting in Xi'an 11

The Stuttering Emissaries of Turfan 12

Promised Wife 13

Lines in the Sand 14

Ten Years 15

Romance of the Maps 16

Afternoon 17

Dusk 18

Weather Report 19

Twilight 20

Evening 21

Early Dark 22

Insomnia 23

Commodity 24

Before Dawn 25

Mai to the Headwaters 26

Midday 27

Absence of Earth 28

Inheritance 29

Saffron City 30

Traffic Signal 31

Daylight Savings 33

For Anne & Laura...
...because every day is Mother's Day

Requiem for a Headscarf
   ~For Raquel

She brings a little sister with pink socks, her
straight teeth are homemade. They
sit at a round table, separated, to

give the lie to herdsmen and their four prophet's
palms. Kind only to a coarse rump, or lazy and snapping
sand flies, deleting invisible sapphire wings. One

by one, separately. They
shift their packs from center to side, like hair
hair that is not hair, not fur, just spider's strands, willful and

separating.

Su Li the outlander cooled her jets in the oasis pool. Paper,
scissor, rock, pliant tiles and
cardboard heatshields. The girl

with the long long hair—to her bone beltbuckle—
and darker than uninhabited coastline than night sky.
Dark like charred wood chairbacks and cloisonne partitions. She

is separate from the rest,
the travelers. We cut our hair
long ago long

before we left.

Tian Mei figured she'd set her hair
on fire. Just bow
her smooth brow into the autumn

firepit, there.
That'll do it.
Fierce. Rage. All

aglow.

When they are sick—or old—women are made
to cut their hair. Thinning and straw stick dry or
greying and unmanageable or greying
and unsightly or dyed to match

an overripe eggplant. So now—now cut now—not fashion.
No. Just flat and blunt or fringed or
shaved the hair equivalent
to ombre. To liberate the skin

the vein, unmask and sequester the main
artery in the neck or
the throat's grotto with its inflatable
scar, its epithelial zipper.

They cut their hair to anticipate
the surgeon, to expedite
the anesthetist, to finesse a finer fit
for the procedural cap.

Should I let my hair down now let
it grow down
for
now?

The Sleep Songs

Ten years passed since she slipped to sleep, she
left and left you pacing the sleep miles, she
knew the stone and sand, the storied red desert, she

knew to avoid the opal dunes. She
sleeps between the corridors of seeded tomato, the other
subterranean vegetables, the roots. Did you

imagine remorse to be so particulate?

The unfurnished arguments, the milk and meats in years
of mammal extravagance, crib to table to bed to board, the animal
famine in leap years asking where to eat, what and where to live
        and what,

where to place the horsehide sofa, the foxfur hammock, what hook
        to hang
the tribal robe. Where does reconciliation take shape? Recollection
        in intimacies
of personal smell: faded hairline and the thin flesh of inner arm.
        On what hut wall

to study the image of one other solitary suicide?

Sleeping under your roof, where night latitudes
zigzag between capillaries and route
the practiced paths of oxygen and someone's

morning toast. Just
in the next room, so no coordination
of muscle and slack skeleton—still

the ceiling holds the matched blood,
the predictions, tendencies and
thirty-nine maternal generations.

The rain left your umbrella drying,
unnecessary. I shrug it shut and sleep—
its bright pattern backdrops

bright-still dream logic, wonderment. Where
will you go? Will it rain?
Surety—

just the sure knowledge that each day we race
the sun west, breathless for our lives—imperceptible.
Yet sure. We trespass the loud, buried sand

sure to merge with the promised mirage.
Messiah
of thirsty tongues.

Tirza & The Black Sisters

Tirza and the Black Priests' School.
Tirza and the black-moled snarl confiscating a swirling effigy.
     Black
the Black Sisters with hands
of bone. *Inshallah.*

Tirza beds the doll beneath mean muslin.
Eyes the line of needle's pierce, the thread
that relieves the plainness. The sleeve's wormhole
she

believes hideout enough. The red
skirt rubbed holy, fingered
currant jelly-jam by thumb chased. The bright
black

forbidden hair bareheaded. Red the lips, red
the swirl, Andalusian traces
of tamarind and cumin, lost traces
of arabesque.

En route from Cordoba pack-riding the muscle of mule's
haunch, the atoms of merchant's miles eroding
doll-feet, the fake flat heels, the lost
shoes.

The sand bats that flirted with earlobes gone
to ground beneath Kunlun dun and dust.
The bright red, the exotic bird's flutter, slap-facing the yellow
desert.

Tirza cocoons the residue, the dyed remainder,
the hand's recall of fabric, the flat Sevillian feet, the red
of red
remembered.

Tirza and the Black Priests' School.
Tirza and the black-moled snarl. Black
the Black Sisters with hands
of bone. *Allahu akbar.*

Dust. Sand. Earth. Silence.

Nature is silent. But only for a time. The bark
of caged dogs and frazzled herd animals and
animals that bear burdens

bark. The sound of me me
feed me. Where is the sun, where
is the air the food? Feed

me. Where can I find the silence the solace of the
caravan? The trek through
silent desert, needle-strewn layers

of earth. The elements call
sing their circumference.
Me. Sing me. Silence the loud

sand.

Hope Is a Thing with Guidelines

1.

By now Alice Lin, the hungry ghost
reconnoitering where the slipshod waves
of St. Augustine runners run where a wedding once

was. Invincible.

Invisible in the spearheads' rustle, she reads
how mitochondrial cell mates would pair
each with blind longing—layered thick like lab slides and shelved

just so, so

two or three or
more ingenious screen names or perforated
avatars could co-

exist.

She watches for the white satin foot, the moss-blurred step,
the body-on-body jubilation—the sweetheart table
flounced over by the diaphanous

bride.

She is there then too, and parabolic
in Swarovski, and now soon, it will be her
turn, her time to repurpose and

retrofit.

2.

At what point along the x axis did Alice Lin—seduced—meet
the grunts, the foreknowing red-headed
tangle of it all?

To second

guess the weather's chest-held
hand, the overdrawn cup
of seismic tea? To be the designated

Sybil

of androgynous soothsayers, tracing petroglyphs
on sheet rock, onto phonelines left
unsecured.

The moment

lost amid the chatter—hums and fits—French
braided tweets, their hashtags zig
zagging. Thumb punch

up

wind and down slope along the Konsu Corridor:
Alice Lin's carbon footprint
in the dry season.

Shut

off the browser trail and power down. Summer
is always anxious always hot. This even the ambidextrous
lizard knows, in balance on a mute asparagus fern.

Even

the left-behind mockingbird with drooping
splayed wing knows, the odd scuttle worms brandishing
their coiled exoskeletal postures must

know.

They rule the day—overseeing
what she overlooked. The humidity
is tolerable by sundown. No records set, no records

broken.

Starting in Xi'an

Their dressmaker's dust-veil is always the same old script,
the redundant mosaic. Step

through any silk window, a corner
rubbed smooth by handprints—erased brick of foundry

the choke of ash and oxidized iron. Improbably,
rainy season came too early. A side exit

known to few already crowded with gliding arms
no stranger to henna's short-lived fade. A female voice

with a country accent. Camel hip-joints unfold
and the hooves fly to gallop between night window's ledge

and the gates of Xi'an. Already bodies
out of body jog the battle yards, board

the snub-nosed ferries, waiting for one idling ignition
to catch, turn the corner. The toll route,

familiar as skin's protein smell,
unfamiliar, as well, but stirring, stirring, stirring

and heartlessly unmapped
and heartlessly non-negotiable.

The Stuttering Emissaries of Turfan

The winding sheets and turbans they stay tucked mostly. Costumed
    order.
And there is ample space and steep shade by the tent folds. Dry tongues
    like dune locusts
click. The baristas set to strong tea-brew your first cardamom swallow.
    They work

the booths, the patio tables surgically, fingerprints smudge
the honeyed ant-trails, the night's sad rehearsals of absinthe and
    sesame seed.
Linseed oil and old shellac. Knobbed fingers they still work folding

unfolding, unmarried mute sisters clawed as ginger root, come sullen
    and sore-knuckled
to burr the wool-tight carpets, virginal pink and by now, loom-ready.
    They work
the crowd stippled after sun damage, sharp-cut the indigo rough, the
    sky-

glazed tiles. Some work the roof of spring days, some sweat
the fault line root, adding heat to the gathering traffic,
the arguing tarmac, adding salt sweat to the silica sand, glaze-blasted

and hypnotized these thousands of reluctant footfalls later. By now,
    you will have
spoken. Desert tried. Taklimakan proud.
Taklimakan proved. The peacocks of sundown. Eerie, dust-loud

and Homeric.

Promised Wife

The way there, Borte rode. She sat high—
the failed bench, the saddle
pinch-backing.

Only later, a horse maybe steppe-bred or small yak
bucking the midday demons, the clowns
of noon, the phase

of day's miles truncated. She looked
sideways, no, not on the mountains or
Burkhan Khaldun in the clouds at her vision's

edge, but shot her small slipstream smile
at Temujin with his long braids, coffee bright
his stare and jagged with hot spikes, acidity

and the flavor of oiled hair and
lust, too, all
so serious, untraveled but for now

and fine spun, too,
the virgin thread.

Lines in the Sand

The false day knew rough work, labored
and urging along the meat,
the multitudes. *Aleppo*. Simply

an unpronounceable name still east
of the River Amu Darya. The meal mouths
complained in jagged sighs

and the meat thighs ached, the unsteady
elevation. Lin
struggled

counting his breath
s.

Ten Years

It took Alice Lin ten years after planting, after
her tribe of cats washed so many
generations, there was no genomic memory, after

all the swallow-flying distance between
the plateaus ankle-deep and east of summer and
the aggressive spice markets to find

her mother. She traveled below
our feet and finally found
the familiar earth liberally laced

with maternal air—yeast flour
and raisins and
walnuts hard

on the teeth
the tongue.

Romance of the Maps

Only those whose feet have felt the slight
rise, the crosswords where known land marks crow's
feet, last spring's washed gully becomes

the place to turn south, leave for once
this unmarked blank and begin
the lookout for oasis emerging

from asphalt from tarmac, a push
of sand, heading not heading in
to the place where trees roost

observing protocols, folding and unfolding.

If you fold the map there at the worn crease, only
the higher elevations are visible, only
the peaks of Kunlun, the foothills

of Appalachia or the Adirondacks,
where bound heels sink arrowheads,
residue

of smoked game, a biblical offering favoring
one son
over another.

Afternoon

Sin Jin's old master belabored the ecstasies of death, the
final shout, appeal to sun storms for more
hydrogen, more. The sun

lived by desert trails. Farther,
from each old man's litany of regret, too little
love, too many days of fingers dulled

by the counting house. Their choices creep forward,
each day their tally. The tired
joints and dark kitchens, eyes

dry, unable
to
shut

even the old male cat moves
slowly to his water
bowl.

Dusk

A younger sister made it her habit to sing
to her mother's bones. Twice yearly
when the summer escaped on an outgoing tide when
the full moon of seething green raised grass heads. The bones

that housed her replicating cells shifted, knew
her steps, her sandaled feet—turning once
to recollect the cadence, they met: one voice
instructing the next.

Weather Report

They tell us grandfather went back
to China. He won't be back. They tell
us, "We had some rain here."

"Here, the front just came in."

One last act of housekeeping before departing Dandan Oilik. The
           desert
promised little
in the way of cabinetry.

Small porcelain knobs, utilitarian shoeboxes
emptied of soft slippers. Here was
one old residue of daywear, pointless now

the lost blush and peony, somewhere gone east
with the housewife of shelved moisture,
sweat stains beneath the ribcage

the small of a back. This
would shroud Mei-tai. Left
with the unborn

fetuses, the waxed lilies.

Twilight

Her obsession became full-bodied
and round—a melon straight
from the tilted garden tracing

the lowland's curve. The silt-heavy
rivers helped carry her throat's sore lump
along, careening rock to rock, riverbed

to tired tributary. Even slogging these foothills,
distant Loulan no more than nightmare
than memory, she nursed each sour swallow.

A stunted child fed on gruel, barely
grain, barely milk, barely
water and redolent with clanging insects.

Evening

Rough fingers probe the sleeping mats
and their party blossoms, a
grandmother's wide-lipped poppies, a bluebell
someone's demure nod. Three chairs, four-

legged, unknown tree anonymous stain, someone
thought the finish moneyed, even
resplendent. Were there water rings marring
the side tables? Someone's night sweats

a shadow for May flowers? Someone
could furnish a newlywed's first hut, if only
the dusty sheets would be
silent.

Early Dark

The dreaming tigers spread their feral sweat, coy atoms
homesteading the unmapped air
complete with flowerbeds

and charcoal grill. The lead walkers known, knew
the middle ground. So long
as they walked, kicked dust and

sand, neutralized pheromones and phlegm in dry throats
clearing. At night, she heard
her name, corners rounded by sleep, a potted plant

where wall met floorboard. Her name. The rest
the slang of private augurs
untranslatable.

Insomnia

Between starpoints she realized lying
bareback on the cold sand, drew
the heat from spinal tissue, from muscle's

ligature, sure sign nothing died nothing sank
toward stasis. The heat circuited through flesh points to
ground crust, silica's endpoint, her

nighttime's entropy. Lying
against cold leather against animal
skin, pressed back toward sofa bed back,

she gathered lingering twigs, somnambulist
counting cards, backward
toward fields toward mountains, how

the land mapped how
middle age played her luck
her hand.

Commodity

Outside the Kunlun Pass, An-Lee knew a man, she
said tall, like the cliché and greying, females
and click beetles, the ambush

of honey mead, sparkle
in a drowsing eyelash. Her knees
felt cold to the touch, legs below the knee

cool. Unshaven and the rub of nylon—eyes
always watched the fabric press
press along the salt, the ochre sand.

Before Dawn

What with May and the drying grasses, prelude
to what desert months will reap and belittle
what cheap coverings and harnesses made dreary

with inadequacy. In the high plains, straw ground only
mumbled the temporary and worthless, the
sniff of green somewhere absent, the sniff

the high speed ailerons bearing down a wet
washing. We poke at
the unintentional remainders. Food

for random nomads, and those who let loose
their home flocks, clowders, covens, assorted
gaggles of new geese bearing down.

The dog-eared remnants,
the dry spring.

Mai to the Headwaters

Mai and I fingered stained
glass geometries. Triangular
wedding sets of pure sunstone

fitting each to one, then
prying down rough
prongs. We liked the hand

of it. The lines of honeycomb,
the virgin blue, the citrus.

Midday

Colorblind on a mountain road. Lin
reshaped his iris diameter, looking
for a break in the fog. Green

seemed a resuscitation of lowland fields, the
terraced markings of family and
truculent neighbors. But green

nonetheless, and green's white-haired grandmother,
green's fragrant newborn, sharp with placental residue,
spring green's flirtatious sister, she

who lost a tooth, no one knows how. The blue shadows
where grass had been chewed raw by stealthy creatures and
their furtive intentions. All

cool color
fog
warmed.

Absence of Earth

They bury the dead in the mountain
on a slant facing the freelane, sightless eye
attracting the sun. The mounds

don't rise, no need when the rough old earth
urges its own elevations. No straight lines
in nature, nothing

but curves along the treeline, the crow's trajectory. How
deep do they need to dig to find
the forest crib, root's cradle?

Inheritance

Alice Lin recognized her grandmother's dress, though
the armholes gaped vacant and the tea-garden
figurines along the hem talked to

themselves, no legs long and veined
listening. The rag pack folded and
unfolded, more strictly to compress the particolored

mixed bag, patterns, prints, plaids, outsqueezed
the spring air from the coastal fields
the furrows. Here

the chest buttons
carried
their own tune.

Saffron City

Karakum ground shifts forward, *says there's more*
to my breath than sand. Those gaudy trees, that hot yellow. The sign.

The sprig. The tabebuia not
pronounced as it seems. The spring. So

amorous, such buttercup leaves, such
gauze, such wounds, such striated tissue.

They neglect to cipher the sun, the stove's
element. The origin. Yellowface

defines the sky, the spleen. The warning. Yellow
colored her skin's jaundice. So Windsor blue

they handpainted her dress. The fake.
The yellow the sign, the signpost

of Gaochang on the outskirts.
Rest the pollen-flecked eyelids, rest

the eyes that ate apricots, the apples and peaches.
The dunes a wanton's back, a fan-dancer's muscled calf.

Flesh and yellow ochre and
the tang of ox-fur's musk,

meat juice on jaw, on
iridescent whiskers.

Traffic Signal

A source of relief. And
quaint.
Shin-ya's mother would order

the downturning world
by reading signs. She'd circle
the vacant square in Xi'an, alphabetize

the menus, configure the dialogues overheard,
the conjoined signals. Cunning how precious
argot would press for her its linear way along

the declarative sentence, its matrix
of ley lines and thunderheads over the desert. And vertical
as the Kunlun peaks, abrupt syntax, a choir's

punctuation and end stop. To be—
and the body, noon day's dreamt arcana of codes
and chemistry, dragging the traveler ever

on and forward. The body—the scared
recalcitrant dog.

Behind her and seven steps back,
the sand mites
the carnal hawk's flight overheard, like

monsters of breath, a month's saliva residue in a dry mouth,
scorched bed pillow invisible, immediate, burred
in the scalloped dunes that lie ahead

the voice only, and young
for the date in fragrant Samarkand—and swaddled
in lucky yellow sleeves, she would

catch a glimpse. Birds
summon, fingers
gesture, the cohort of rose attar, there

there, the wordless young
intone.

Daylight Savings

It was the cheat time, the fox months and weeks.
Water moccasin belching after feathers and beak. Even
the hours are compromised. From the coy sneer

that destabilizes—she likes the smirk—
to the jarring single
sign. She sings,

the belt, the rub of steel on steel singes
sting
s.

C.M. Clark's poetry has appeared nationally in a variety of publications, including *Metonym Literary Journal, The Lindenwood Review, Dogwood: A Journal of Poetry & Prose, Painted Bride Quarterly, the South Florida Poetry Journal* and *Gulf Stream* magazine, as well as the 10th Anniversary *Tigertail Anthology* of South Florida writers (Fall 2013). New work will soon be appearing in the upcoming anthology *Travellin' Mama*. Clark was runner-up for the Slate Roof Press 2016 Chapbook Contest and Elyse Wolf Prize. Her most recent collection, *Dragonfly*, was released by Solution Hole Press in late 2016.

Previously, Clark participated in programs featuring contemporary American poets at the Miami Book Fair. She also served as inaugural Poet-in-Residence at the Deering Estate Artists Village in Miami, resulting in the collection, *Charles Deering Forecasts the Weather & Other Poems* (Solution Hole Press, 2012). Prior collections include *The Blue Hour* (Three Stars Press, 2007), and the artbook *Pillowtalk*, with painter Georges LeBar. Clark has a Ph.D. in English from the University of Miami, and teaches writing and literature at Miami Dade College.